Silk & Venom

Searching for a Dangerous Spider

For Greta Binford and Father Dale
K. L. and C. G. K.

First edition 2011

Library of Congress Cataloging-in-Publication Data is available.

Library of Congress Catalog Card Number pending

ISBN 978-0-7636-4222-8

10 11 12 13 14 15 16 SCP 10 9 8 7 6 5 4 3 2 1

Printed in Humen, Dongguan, China

This book was typeset in Optima.

Candlewick Press
99 Dover Street
Somerville, Massachusetts 02144

visit us at www.candlewick.com

Silk & Venom

Searching for a Dangerous Spider

Kathryn Lasky ◉ photographs by **Christopher G. Knight**

CANDLEWICK PRESS

Survivors

Spiders are old. They have survived on the earth for at least 400 million years. That's four hundred times as long as humans. Spiders were here before dinosaurs. And when dinosaurs vanished, almost 65 million years ago, spiders lived on.

One millionth or even a billionth the size of a dinosaur, with fangs thousands of times smaller than a *Tyrannosaurus rex*'s tooth, spiders have their own defenses. By means of silk and venom, they have flourished.

More than forty thousand species of spiders have been discovered so far. And scientists are still finding new ones. Some sand spiders can camouflage themselves in any color sand, and some water spiders spin silken air bubbles to make their own scuba tank–style nests beneath the surface of lakes or ponds. There are even spiders that live in snow and ice!

The biggest error anyone can make about spiders is to call them insects. Spiders do belong to the same phylum, or group, as insects: they are both arthropods, a category that includes everything from spiders and ants to shrimp and crabs. It is not an especially exclusive group. All you need for admission is a segmented body, an external skeleton, and jointed limbs.

These tyrannosaurus teeth are much smaller than actual size.

abdomen

cephalothorax

But within the arthropod phylum, there is another, smaller group: arachnids. Arachnids include spiders, scorpions, daddy longlegs, mites, and ticks. The main feature of arachnids is that unlike other arthropods, which have three major body parts—the head, chest, and abdomen—arachnids have only two. In arachnids, the head and the chest section (called the thorax) are fused into one part, called the cephalothorax. A spider's cephalothorax contains its brain, venom glands, and sucking stomach. A spider's abdomen contains its heart, more of its digestive system, and its spinning glands.

Another important feature of arachnids is that while insects have three pairs of legs, arachnids have four or more. In fact, most have six pairs of leglike appendages, not all of which are for walking. At first glance these appendages seem to be attached every which way. Toward the front of the head are two appendages that on males look like mini boxing gloves and on females like little legs. These are called pedipalps. In males the "palps" are used for reproductive purposes. In front of the pedipalps are two more appendages that are adapted for feeding and defense. These are called chelicerae, and at their tips, like two dark eyes, are the fangs. The fangs can fold away neatly when not in use.

So, body parts and leg counts distinguish spiders and other arachnids from insects. What makes spiders different from their fellow arachnids—daddy longlegs, mites, and such? Silk and venom. Spiders have spinnerets for producing silk and can use their fangs to inject venom.

The spiders on these two pages are orb weavers.

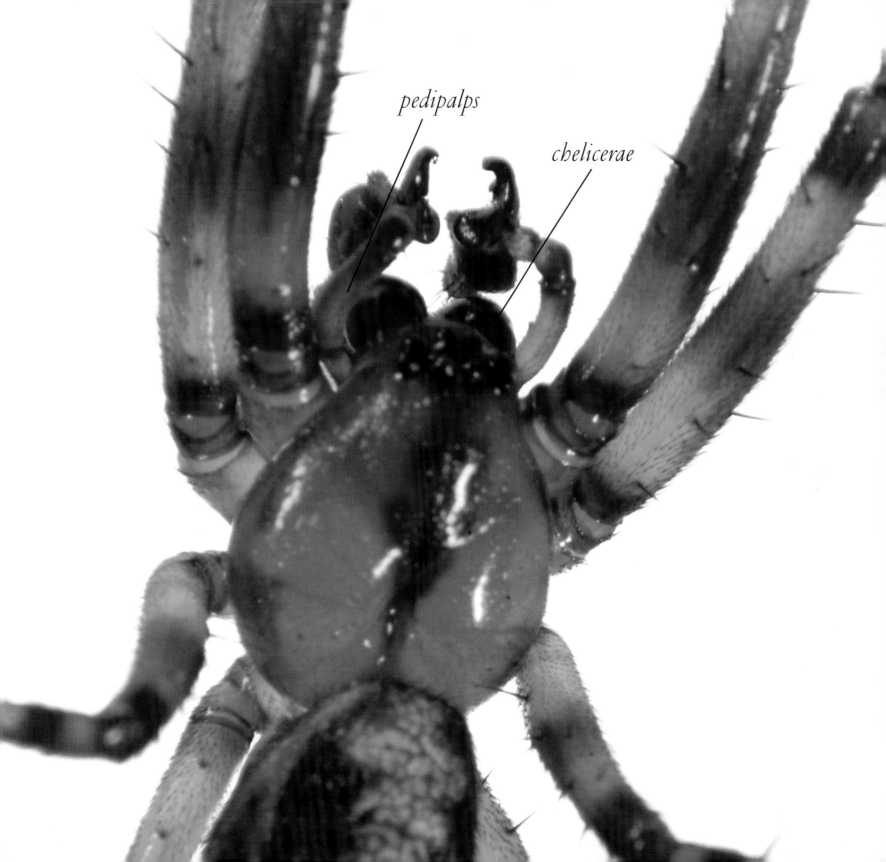

pedipalps

chelicerae

Top: A funnel web

Bottom: A spiny orb weaver suspended in its web

Opposite page: A garden spider wrapping a newly caught moth in silk

Spiders produce several different kinds of silk, each with its own purpose. They use capture silk for binding up prey and dragline silk for the outer edges of a web. Females even make a special silk just for constructing egg sacs. And ballooning spiders make a kind of silk that forms a thready parachute, helping them soar through the air.

Not only are spiders tricked out with all kinds of silk-making capabilities, but they also have a secret weapon: venom. When a spider bites its prey, its fangs inject a powerful venom that paralyzes the victim. Next, the spider vomits into the puncture wounds made by the fangs. The spider's digestive juices then immediately begin to dissolve the prey's innards into liquid so they can be sucked into the spider's stomach. Slurp!

Spiders have one more little trick. Although spiders can have as many as eight eyes, most spiders don't depend on their vision but on another sense organ: the sensitive hairs on their legs, which they use to detect and decode vibrations. Sometimes a male will use this code in courtship rituals, sending a message to a female by drumming its web. But the vibratory signals are also vital to capturing prey. Perched on the silken threads of its web, a spider can feel and distinguish the vibrations emitted from the passing wingbeats of a butterfly, the footfalls of an ant, or the buzz of a fly. The web can ensnare prey, but it is still possible for the creature to escape. So the spider must be alert—no sleeping on the job! The second a prey animal is trapped in its web, the spider picks up the message and pounces on its victim.

The ability to adapt to a wide variety of habitats. A tool kit filled with an array of silks. Venomous fangs. And sensitive, hairy legs. Put it all together, and you've got a survivor: the spider.

The Thinking Tree

Spiders have great patience. They can wait for hours quietly, unmoving. They are masters of stillness—in a dust-clotted attic, a dirt-encrusted abandoned car, a woodpile. Some are quite fond of filth and find great comfort in crud.

Greta Binford is patient, too, and in pursuit of a spider, she does not mind the filth. She is an arachnologist, a professor of biology at Lewis and Clark College in Portland, Oregon.

When she was a little girl, growing up on a farm in Indiana, Greta Binford didn't talk much. She watched. She watched things very carefully and up close.

She would crawl on her hands and knees right behind the tractor as her dad plowed the fields. She observed with amazement every little creature that wriggled out from the upturned earth. She would pick up a worm, a stinkbug, or a giant ant, then hold it carefully, turn it over, let it slither and skitter on her hand or scale up her arm to her elbow, then gently put it back into the soil.

"She sure was a regular pigpen—dirty all the time," says her dad, chuckling. "She just loved looking deep, really deep, at nature."

Her family's farm was Greta's world. The land included a creek, whose banks concealed a variety of fossils, as well as geodes, which she liked to crack open, and a great swimming hole. And overhanging the creek's banks was a special tree. She called it her thinking tree. She would climb up into the limbs of this tree to escape the growl of tractors, slams of doors, or any human-made sounds. In summer and spring, the air was strung with birdsong and the hum of bees. Through the green lacy embroidery of summer leaves, she could see upstream, across the creek, and over to a marsh with all sorts of wildlife. She called it her thinking tree because as she looked out on the landscape, her mind became tranquil, and she could think about all sorts of things.

Some of her thoughts were everyday thoughts about school and family. She would think about cheerleading, whispering the cheers and imagining the jumps and moves to go with them. She thought about gymnastics and running track. She thought about the mean trick her older brother played on her when he had put kitten chow in a bowl and said it was a new kind of cereal. She took one bite and blew it out, splattering everything around her.

But Greta thought about more unusual things as well. She watched the dragonflies skimming the creek below and wondered why they had two sets of wings. She thought about the latest geode she had found. Every geode she had ever cracked open revealed an inner world of crystals and color as dazzling as any fantasy empire.

She often looked for arrowheads and Native American beads along the creek banks with friends. "I felt a real connection with the North American Indians," she says, "and through that, a connection with the woods." It fueled Greta's sense of wonder to think that both she and some of the first Americans had walked over the same rocks, looked upon the same creek, and observed the same details of this woodland.

Greta and her father walk the banks of the creek on the Binford farm.

In ancient time, long before any humans ever walked through these woods, the land that is home to Greta's family farm was very different from the way it is today. One does not think of oceans in the middle of America, but once, more than 400 million years ago, a shallow sea lapped where there is now a creek, and today, along the creek banks, one can find fossils of sea life. After the sea evaporated, the fossil imprints of crinoids (long-extinct sea lilies), saltwater clam shells, and other mollusk shells lay like secrets buried in sediment that built up over millions upon millions of years. Then, a mere two hundred thousand years ago, three glaciers pushed down through the Midwest into southern Indiana, scraping up the earth and peeling back the layers of sediment to reveal the hidden life that existed at the time of this ancient sea. The fossils reveal sea life that now would never be found in the fresh gurgling waters of a brook or anywhere near the state of Indiana.

At first, when Greta was still young, she did not think so much about the deep time of the earth's history. That was simply too much time to wrap her mind around. But she especially loved the fossilized sea lilies, the crinoids, and wondered about that ancient sea. Were there sharks? Wading apatosauruses? Over time, as she studied the natural world around her, she began to feel more comfortable with the biological explanations of the earth's development than with a literal view of the ones in the Bible. She questioned how God could have done it all in just seven days. Greta believed that maybe God needed more time to make such an exciting, diverse world of living things. Maybe he wasn't even finished yet! Maybe it wasn't all over! For Greta, letting go of the Bible stories did not mean letting go of God. It was simply another way to look closely at nature, with wider eyes and a broader mind. She would need this wide view of life if she was to be a scientist.

Greta had been studying to become a high-school science teacher when a professor asked if she wanted to go to Peru to help out on a spider expedition. A free trip to South America was attractive. Once there, her job was to sit and watch rare rainforest spiders that live in a huge communal web—hundreds of thousands of spiders working together to build and maintain their home. Greta was to observe how they cooperated in building the web and in catching prey.

By the time she made her way back to camp each evening, it was dark in the jungle. But she wasn't frightened. She was too excited to be scared. For Greta had found an incomparable beauty in the spiders and how they worked together. When she returned from South America, she changed her major from education to zoology, the study of animals. In particular, she studied how the vast diversity of spiders, and the chemicals in them, evolved to be so different from one another. This started a particular interest in a species well known for the chemicals in its venom, *Loxosceles reclusa,* more commonly known as the brown recluse. And Greta did not have to go to foreign countries to find a close relative.

In fact, it was a big surprise when someone discovered that the Indiana statehouse was infested with *Loxosceles rufescens,* the Mediterranean brown spider, a venomous relative to the recluse. The spiders apparently had moved into the basement just beneath the statehouse's rotunda and found a comfy habitat in the auditor's files, the files that keep track of all the money the state spends and receives. Often, a department in the statehouse needed to review these records, and so they would be sent up to offices on the various floors. Soon there were brown spiders running around all over the place, as busy as any statehouse employee.

Greta happened to be in Indiana when she heard about the infestation. She was terribly excited—until she got there and discovered that the exterminators had already been called in. Although she was disappointed, a part of her was sympathetic. She knew people would panic. But she also knew that the Mediterranean brown spider was misunderstood. People could not comprehend that these spiders are solitary, shy, and even docile by nature. They bite only in self-defense. Yes, they could kill a patch of your skin, but they would prefer to kill something more their own size that they could digest.

Most bites to humans happen at night, when a person is sleeping and accidentally squishes a spider that gets into the bed. No one slept at the

Greta as a college student on her first big expedition in Peru

statehouse, so the chances of someone being bitten were small. But Greta imagined that accidents could happen if someone was looking for a report in a file drawer and encountered a brown spider all cozy between the papers.

Despite the work of the exterminator, there were still several live spiders crawling about in the cracks and crevices in the basement. Somehow this toxic spider had arrived in America from its native countries around the Mediterranean Sea, survived an exterminator, and seemed to have a preference for municipal buildings with comfy filing cabinets and old records!

For Greta, the distinction of whether spiders are in a region naturally (and so are native to that region) or have been brought there by human transport (and so have been introduced) is important. The spiders in the statehouse were certainly introduced.

Two Loxosceles *spiders related to those that invaded the Indiana statehouse*

A Family Reunion

Some years after the statehouse infestation, Greta returns to southern Indiana for a family reunion at a state park. With a passel of young cousins, nieces, and nephews trailing behind her, she leads them on a spider hunt. She wants to share her enthusiasm for spiders and show these kids how spiders are absolutely everywhere!

She carries with her a plastic baseball bat and a "beat sheet"—a square frame with fine gauze netting stretched between the four sides. She puts the frame down beneath a bush, and the kids begin to beat the bush for spiders. At least a dozen fall onto the white square of netting—jumping spiders, crab spiders, many kinds of orb weavers—none of which is poisonous or aggressive. The kids scoop them up in small plastic vials for a closer look. Then they release them.

Next, the kids follow Greta along a path into the woods. On the way, they find a funnel web moored to a crack in the rocks above the creek. On the porch of its cone is an *Agelenopsis*. In the silk bordering the *Agelenopsis* is a tiny orb web of the *Uloborus*, one of the few spiders that kills its prey by wrapping it so tightly it dies.

Along a creek's banks, sparkling on the rock ledges, they pick out the silvery filaments of spiderwebs quivering on a windless summer day. There might be as many as two dozen different species of spiders along the creek and in the woods. Resting on a pad of moss, like a small lace bowl, is the web of a linyphiid, a sheet-web-weaving spider. Strung in the shrubbery of the higher part of the banks, the radial disks of countless orb weavers glitter in the dappled light of the woods. Closer to the water, a web stretches like a fishnet across the rocks. It belongs to a *Tetragnatha*, another orb weaver. These particular spiders either sit on their webs or perch, usually in a rock crack, with a thread of silk attached to their webs and wait patiently for a low-flying insect—a water skimmer, perhaps a dragonfly or a mosquito—any bug that is drawn to watery places.

All of these creek-bank spiders feel the footfalls of the approaching creatures—Greta and her gang. But the thumps that vibrate through the silk, setting the nano-hairs on their legs aquiver, immediately signal that this is neither prey nor predators drawing near. The children are impressed with all the spiders they have found in such a short time, and Greta is careful to explain how spiders have no interest in them. Spiders are practical. "They pick on something their own size," she says, and explains that they do not prey on anything that is too big for them to paralyze, liquefy, and digest.

The next day on the Binford farm, Greta returns to her thinking tree to look for more spiders in the bushes nearby. She is hoping to find a spitting spider. There are more than 150 different kinds of these spiders, which go out from their webs to seek their prey. When a spitting spider finds a possible victim, it takes aim and then flicks its jaws from side to side, making a *Z* pattern with its gooey, venomous spit to tether its insect target. It will then stab its victim with its fangs. But there are no spitters in sight today. There is, however, a beautiful orb weaver, *Leucauge,* as colorful as an Easter egg.

Not more than a quarter of a mile from the creek is the old barn that Greta and her brother used to play in. The barn has a feeling of abandonment. It is a place to stockpile rusted equipment and old furniture. Vines crawl right up the walls and creep inside through hayloft windows and roof cracks. There is a 1976 Honda Civic festooned with spiderwebs. The muddy footprints of a raccoon leave clear tracks across the windshield. The inside of the car is a total mess, with mouse nests and more spiderwebs in the ripped-up cushions of the backseat.

There has been plenty of spider activity in the old barn. High up near a hayloft window is the glittering radial web of an orb weaver. It is quite different from anything a brown recluse would weave. Brown recluse webs tend to be messy, tangled affairs. They are loosely woven, and their silk is very sticky, ideal for trapping prey if an insect passes by during the day. They are also a pale blue-gray. Most often, however, brown recluses go out and hunt at night. Greta has followed them. But not when she was a little kid. According to her brother, Greta was afraid of the dark. She had to fall in love with spiders as a college student on her first expedition to Peru to get over that fear.

A barn full of treasures: the ancient Honda Civic, a funnel weaver hunkered down in rotting wood, and an orb weaver's web

Cracking the Code

Because spiders are almost a half a billion years old, Greta wonders where they started out on earth and how they got to where they are now. To understand these issues better, she has had to learn about the geographical history of the earth and its continents.

Since the time of Galileo, we have known that the earth moves around the sun. However, for an even longer time people believed that the earth's continents were firmly anchored to the seafloors. But this is not so. Plate tectonics is the study of the earth's plates, or crusts, and the large-scale movement of these huge hunks of land. This science has revealed that once, more than a billion years ago, there was one supercontinent, which scientists now call Rodinia.

This supercontinent began to break up, and big chunks drifted away like floating puzzle pieces scattered on a huge pond. Some collided with each other to form new continents, including the supercontinent of Pangaea. Then over time, millions and millions of years, *these* continents began to crack and break. Chunks, wedges, slices, and blocks floated off in all directions.

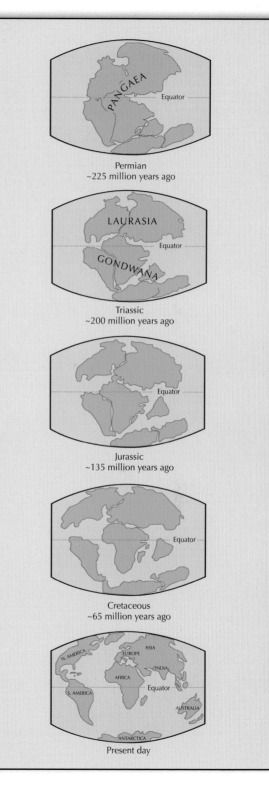

Permian
~225 million years ago

Triassic
~200 million years ago

Jurassic
~135 million years ago

Cretaceous
~65 million years ago

Present day

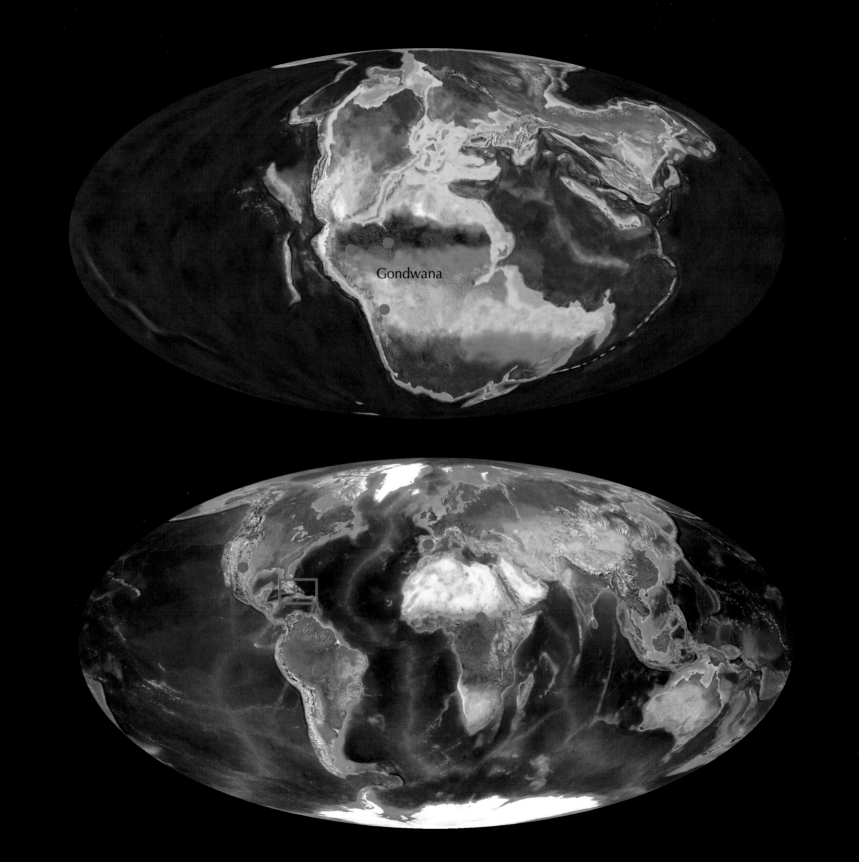

Gondwana

Nothing stayed put! Nothing was anchored. But there were spiders on Pangaea, and when it fractured, the spiders became separated and were distributed all over the world. Each community of spiders had to adjust to the circumstances of its new environment in order to fit in and survive.

The story of what became Greta's favorite spiders, *Loxosceles,* began, she learned, in Gondwana, the supercontinent that at one time included South America, Africa, India, Australia, New Zealand, and Antarctica. There are now one hundred species of *Loxosceles* in the world. She thinks that these spiders came from western Gondwana, because now most of them are found in Africa, South America, and North America. She believes that the first *Loxosceles* made it from South America to North America before the current land connection through Panama existed. That connector, the Isthmus of Panama, has been there for only three million years, and Greta is testing a hypothesis that the spiders crossed from South America to North America 33 to 35 million years ago. "It's not a simple story," Greta says.

But how does one find out the answers to this un-simple story? How does one trace the routes that spiders have taken over hundreds of millions of years? Do they leave behind any signs—logs, maps, diaries? In a sense, yes. It is all written in their DNA and their venom. This is the story that Greta is trying to decipher in her lab.

THROW DEAD TINY BABIES IN THE TRASH. WE DON'T WANT THEM.

This is the first of several instructions on a container labeled DEAD BOX in Greta's lab at Lewis and Clark College. Other notes are posted for students working here, including ONLY SPIDERS EAT IN THE LAB.

Opposite page: The top map shows the supercontinent Gondwana. Red dots indicate possible sites for the original Loxosceles. *The bottom map shows the world as it looks today with the red dots showing where* Loxosceles *are native. The rectangle represents Greta's current search area.*

There are, however, more live spiders in the lab than dead ones. These live spiders are kept in a small sealed room. The temperature is 75°F, with just 45-percent humidity. The environment replicates the climate of an Arizona desert on a wet day, although only a fraction of the eight hundred spiders come from Arizona. There are many from Africa, South America, and Central America.

Each spider has its own private suite. It is a small rectangular plastic box with a hole in the top stuffed with cotton so that some air can come in but the spider can't escape. The spider room reverberates with the constant thrum of the heating and climate-control equipment. Since the spiders are contained, they cannot hunt for their food, but there is room service, so to speak—live crickets are delivered to each occupant once every two or three weeks. The lab orders batches in varying sizes from a biological supply house. The crickets are then dropped into every spider container. So in addition to feeding the spiders, Greta and her students and assistants must feed the crickets.

The spiders in Greta's lab have been collected over a period of seven or eight years. And there are maybe a dozen or more kinds of *Loxosceles* and their relatives. Greta takes out one of her favorites—the "six-eyed sand spider," *Sicarius,* which can be found in both Africa and South America. These spiders have the unique ability to camouflage themselves in any color sand. Greta takes a *Sicarius* from its box and puts it in a larger box full of blue sand so it can demonstrate its particular talent. Within minutes, it has covered itself in the colorful granules that stick to its hairs. It appears completely indistinguishable from the sand.

Greta then feeds another sand spider that has buried itself in another sandbox. With a plastic straw called a pooter, she sucks up a small cricket and then blows it into this second sandbox. Suddenly the spider explodes from the sand and pounces on the tiny cricket. Within a few seconds, the cricket is motionless, paralyzed by the spider's venom. The spider then injects its digestive juices into the cricket, and the cricket's innards begin to dissolve.

Top: Two six-eyed sand spiders that have emerged from contrasting colors of sand

Bottom: A cricket is sucked up by Greta's pooter.

Right: The six-eyed sand spider doesn't thank Greta, but enjoys its cricket dinner.

There are more than one hundred *Loxosceles* species worldwide, with fifty-four known species in North America, Central America, and the Caribbean. Greta is trying to figure out these different spider species' family tree—in short, how they are related to one another. She can unravel their history by unlocking their genetic code, their DNA. Another part of this secret is buried in the venom. The venom also provides a peephole into the evolutionary history of spiders. The venom of a *Loxosceles reclusa* contains more than two hundred different chemical compounds. These compounds short-circuit its victims' nerves, paralyze their limbs, and slow their hearts. They may also begin the flesh-dissolving process.

To get this venom for study, Greta milks the spider's fangs. She has never been bitten in all the years of collecting the spiders or milking their fangs. Milking a poisonous spider requires steady hands. Greta places the spider in a small vial into which she pumps carbon dioxide, a gas, which will put the spider to sleep. Then she removes it from the vial with tweezers. She fixes the tweezers into a set of clamps so her hands can be free.

"Two hands, ten fingers are hardly enough for this," she says. She will also use her foot in a moment. But before that, she hooks up rubber tubing to a hypodermic needle. This is what she calls the vomit vacuum; she will use it to suck up the vomit from the spider's mouth, keeping it away from the venom. In her other hand she holds a microcapillary tube to catch the venom from the fangs. She has attached electrodes to both the tweezers and the vomit vacuum to make a closed electrical circuit. When she presses on a foot pedal underneath the table, the spider receives a small shock. The shock triggers muscle contractions, which cause the spider to vomit and spurt venom. None of this causes the spider any pain since it is knocked out by the carbon dioxide.

Greta will then test the venom to analyze its chemical composition. The venoms of most closely related spider species are similar. But one branch of the *Loxosceles* family tree, in South America, has venom that is quite different from other *Loxosceles*. What happened in its evolutionary path to make the venoms of this branch of the *Loxosceles* family tree so different? To answer this question, Greta pursues two methods of inquiry—venom analysis and the analysis of genes, the spider's DNA. To get their DNA, she will remove a leg from a young spider, which can regrow that leg in a subsequent molt, and then she analyzes its genetic components.

The venom analysis is a chemical mystery complicated by the vomit of the spider. For in both the venom and the vomit, there are chemicals that dissolve tissue, but they are different and work in different ways. There is not a clear division between the chemicals that paralyze a victim and those that dissolve its tissues.

Solving these mysteries will not only help unravel the secrets of the species family tree but may do much more as well. Spider venom is a source of hidden riches, a possible treasure trove from which medical researchers hope not only to create antivenoms for people who are bitten by spiders of the brown recluse family but also to explore other medical uses. For example, researchers are interested in spider venom for the treatment of stroke victims and for pain medications.

Greta uses a microscope to see the details of her milking operation.

Searching

Greta's big questions are how and when *Loxosceles* made it to the North American continent and what the ancestral connection was between these North American spiders and their South American cousins. There are only six species of *Loxosceles* found in the Caribbean, but they are an important part of the puzzle of the *Loxosceles* family tree.

Greta has flown four thousand miles south and east from her laboratory on a collecting expedition.

"Buscamos arañas" ("We are searching for spiders"), Greta says to a fruit vendor in the marketplace in Puerta Plata, a city in the Dominican Republic, on the island of Hispaniola.

Greta describes this as her "spider Spanish." The lady immediately ducks under her table, which is piled high with fruit and vegetables, to take a look. A rooster walks from beneath the table, but that's it.

"¡Nada!" the vendor calls out. *"¡No hay ninguna arañas!"* These words, however, are enough to excite several children and other merchants. Soon half a dozen people are looking around their market stands.

Greta gets down on her hands and knees and begins crawling about. A chicken accompanies her. Greta is wearing a headlamp to peer into the darkest corners, as well as a multi-pocketed vest stuffed with a couple dozen vials in the pockets of one side. If she finds a spider, she will pop it in the vial and transfer it to a pocket on the other side of her vest. On her hands she wears baseball batting gloves. Meanwhile she is lecturing two college students, Alec and Brendan, who have accompanied her on this trip to learn how to collect. She remembers back to her own first trip to Peru and how important it was to have a good feel for what she was looking for and supposed to observe. Therefore, Greta is trying to give these students what she calls a "search image" for where *Loxosceles* might lurk. "Remember, they like dusty, shadowy, dirty places that haven't been disturbed." She does find spiders, just not the kind she wants.

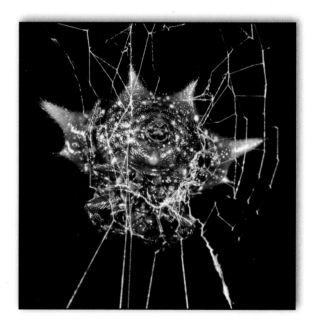

Bottom: A spiny orb weaver spider found in the market

The spiders in the Dominican Republic can help fill in the big picture. Greta's hypothesis is that the ancestors of North American *Loxosceles* crossed over one of the ancient land bridges that existed before the Isthmus of Panama. But she has learned to be very open-minded and entertain other possibilities. For example, it is perfectly possible that there was some kind of reverse migration and that the spiders from North and Central America traveled east and actually are the ancestors of the Caribbean spiders. Up until the time of Greta's trip to the Dominican Republic, there was data for only one species in the Caribbean. It fit the pattern of branching off the base of the North American tree (see the *Loxosceles caribbea* branch on the tree). By obtaining more species in the Dominican Republic, she can compare what she finds and see if indeed this pattern is a general one for all the Caribbean species.

To figure this out, she has to track back in time. The current land connection between South and North America, the Isthmus of Panama, is only three million years old. But there is evidence that the ancestors of those *Loxosceles* of North America predate the isthmus by millions of years, including a twenty-million–year-old fossil found in the Dominican Republic. The shape of the islands was quite different 33–35 million years ago and made a temporary bridge. There are six species of *Loxosceles* in the islands of the Caribbean that are related to those in North America.

Greta is hunting for two species of *Loxosceles* spiders—*Loxosceles cubana* and *Loxosceles taino*. So far, scientists have found *L. taino* only in the dry parts on the south side of the island of Hispaniola. The only record of *L. cubana* on the island is from southern Haiti. Greta hopes to collect the two species in the northwestern deserts of the Dominican Republic.

Loxosceles Branch of the Spider Phylogenetic Tree

LOXOSCELES
95 million years ago

WHAT THE WORLD MIGHT HAVE LOOKED LIKE

GONDWANA

Equator

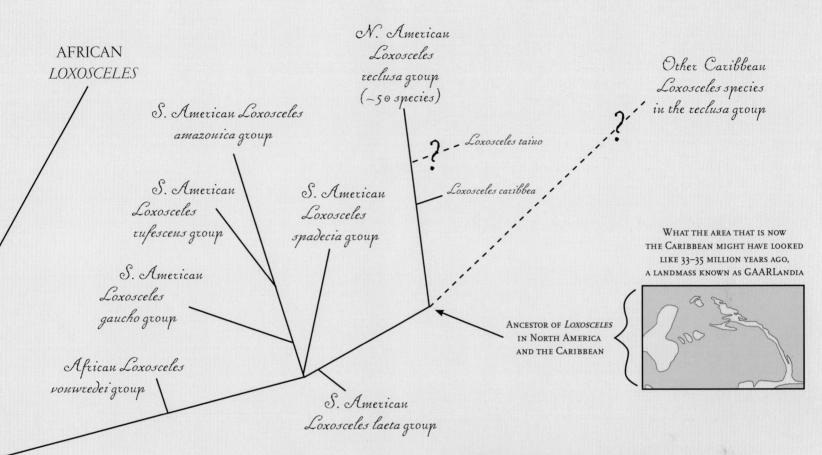

AFRICAN *LOXOSCELES*

S. American Loxosceles amazonica group

N. American Loxosceles reclusa group (~50 species)

Other Caribbean Loxosceles species in the reclusa group

S. American Loxosceles rufescens group

S. American Loxosceles spadecia group

S. American Loxosceles gaucho group

? *Loxosceles taino*

Loxosceles caribbea

African Loxosceles vonwredei group

S. American Loxosceles laeta group

Ancestor of *Loxosceles* in North America and the Caribbean

What the area that is now the Caribbean might have looked like 33–35 million years ago, a landmass known as GAARLandia

This is a family tree of spiders in the genus Loxosceles. The branches of the tree represent connections between spider ancestors and other ancestors, or ancestors and living spiders. The tips where names are written represent living species or groups of species and where they live now. If a branch is dotted, it means Greta thinks that is where those spiders fit in the family tree but this must be tested with data from the spiders she finds in the Dominican Republic.

AREA OF GRETA BINFORD'S RESEARCH

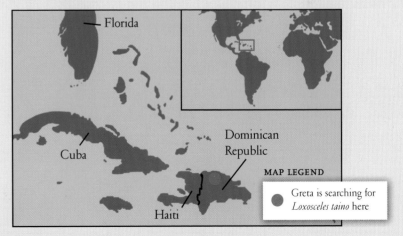

Florida

Cuba

Dominican Republic

Haiti

MAP LEGEND

● Greta is searching for *Loxosceles taino* here

When she crawls out from under the market tables, she looks around at the bustling vendor stands under the corrugated tin roof. There are piles of bananas, guavas, coconuts.

"*¿Conoce alguna casa abandonada?*" she asks the lady. ("Do you know of an abandoned house?") She wants to find something really dilapidated, that has not been disturbed for a long time. Someone points toward another street.

Soon Greta is scrambling over the ruins of an old chocolate factory. There are jagged chinks in the concrete. Cocoa beans are scattered on the cracked pavement of a courtyard. This would seem ideal for *Loxosceles,* who delight in such an environment—the crumbling chaos, the dirt and debris, the mildew under moldering old sheets of roofing—but there is not a one to be seen.

Greta covers a lot of territory in a day. Four hours later, she is near the top of a mountain. She enters a cave and with her headlamp examines the damp rock walls. She takes a pooter from around her neck and sucks up a pholcid, a type of daddy longlegs. She pops it into a vial and tucks the vial into a vest pocket so she can have a closer look at it later. On her trip down the mountain, she wades into a dell of bright pink-and-red ginger. She overturns a rotting log. *Perfect,* she thinks when she finds a *Theridion,* in the same family as the black widow with a fluorescent orange spot.

Her vest pockets are filling up with vials of spiders that may be of interest to other spider researchers, but she hasn't found any *Loxosceles.* At each place she collects, she takes out her battery-powered Global Positioning System to determine the longitude and latitude and writes it on a label she sticks on the vial.

The last stop of the day is in the village of San Marcos. This is a village with no paved streets, no running water, and no electricity. The schools are so small and the children are so many that most children can go to school for only half a day—some in the morning, some in the afternoon. There is not room for them all at the same time. And they walk to school with bare feet, for many do not have shoes.

It is Father Dale, an Eastern Orthodox priest and the director of the Dominican Outreach, a nongovernmental organization, who has led Greta to the village. Dominican Outreach's purpose is to help children like the ones in this small village. Father Dale introduces Greta to his good friend Marie, a teacher without a school.

Marie came to this village several years ago from Haiti. She knows how important education is. In a country where many cannot read or write, she decided to devote her life to teaching the children during the half of the day they are not in regular school. She has been anticipating Greta's visit for weeks, and when Greta arrives, there are almost twenty children crammed on the front porch of Marie's tiny house. There is a blackboard and it has the lesson of the day written in neat letters. But now the children turn around as the special guest, *"la profesora Greta, una profesora de las arañas,"* has arrived. They cheer and clap.

Greta comes up to the front and begins speaking her spider Spanish. The children understand her perfectly. *"¿Cuántas clases diferentes de arañas hay en todo el mundo?"* she asks them. ("In the whole world, how many different kinds of spiders are there?") They ooh and aah with disbelief when she tells them that there are more than forty thousand and that many more remain to be discovered.

"Hay muchas partes del mundo sin explorar, ¡y están esperando que vosotros las descubráis!" ("Much of the world is unknown and waiting to be discovered, waiting for you!") This is the most important thing that Greta tells these children in her spider Spanish.

She then gives them a quick lesson in how to beat a bush with a stick or baseball bat to shake loose the spiders. Soon twenty children are in the tiny yard of Marie's house beating the bushes. Within fifteen minutes, the children have collected more than a dozen different species of spiders. No *Loxosceles*, but a fantastic red-orange spider that looks like a tiny cartoon character. But there is no paint, no art director. It's pure nature!

A Hint of Blue

Greta never panics—even when the brakes fail on the van she is driving as she searches Hispaniola for the elusive *Loxosceles.* "Hey, guys! No brakes." The van rolls to a stop in a village with perhaps five houses total. Two young men arrive to examine the problem. A part is needed. The nearest place to buy the part is an hour away. Father Dale hops on the back of one fellow's motorbike and waves good-bye as he goes off to collect the part. But it's business as usual for Greta. She turns to the old woman whose house is nearest the van and launches into spider Spanish. *"¿Conoce alguna casa abandonada? Buscamos arañas."* The woman is instantly intrigued. *"No hay casas abandonadas, pero ¿quieres dar un vistazo detrás de mi casa?"* she suggests. ("There are no abandoned houses, but would you like to look behind mine?")

The woman leads Greta to her small backyard. Soon others join in. Excitement has come to this small dusty village with this *profesora estadounidense.*

Although there are some spiders in the woman's backyard, none of them are *Loxosceles.* Still, Greta knows that these spiders are out there somewhere on the island of Hispaniola. Nothing stops Greta—not brake failures, not tangled spiny vines, not rutted roads.

Opposite page: The fantastic red-orange Chrysso *spider found by children at Marie's school*

The next day, when the van is fixed, she heads farther west. The first stop is an orphanage, Casa Hogar Amor, where Father Dale introduces Greta to the children.

Carlo, a boy of perhaps nine, immediately joins in as Greta spies a pile of rubbish just behind the orphanage. Carlo discovers a *Leucauge*, one of the multicolored orb weavers. This particular one is as dazzling as a Christmas tree ornament.

"Hey!" Greta says, calmly poking into a hollow concrete building block. "Got a molt of a *Loxosceles* here."

Sure enough, there is the discarded shell of a baby *Lox* that has outgrown its exoskeleton. What makes this molt conspicuously that of a *Loxosceles* is that the legs stick straight out, unlike other spiders' molts. "Sometimes babies hang out together to share food," Greta says, searching the area. But here there are none.

Ten minutes later, in the pit of a nearby old stone quarry, Greta finds the web of a brown widow, then another and another, one with an egg sac in its web.

The quarry is an ugly place, littered with discarded plastic bottles, juice cartons, old mattress springs, rusted cans, tire fragments, and crumpled Styrofoam containers. The prettiest thing in this pit of trash, however, is the egg sac of a "woman who murders husbands," *Latrodectus geometricus*—a brown widow spider! In the crisscross filaments of the silken web, the egg sac drifts like a hazy moon swathed in gauze. Greta picks up the murderess and her precious egg sac and puts them in a vial for a friend who studies them.

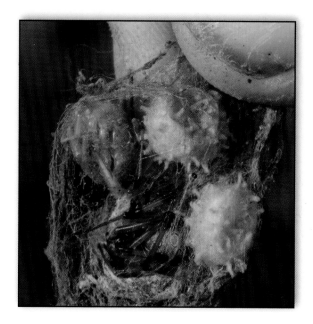

Top: A brown widow (a close relative of the black widow) surveys her territory.

Bottom: Has she misplaced her egg sac? Greta has found it.

That afternoon, Greta drives farther west toward the Haitian border. The country becomes drier. Cactus spike the land that was once an ancient seabed. The delicate branches of acacia trees open like umbrellas under a cloudless sky. Greta pulls the van over. She looks out the window. A light breeze cuts through the pale grass, giving the illusion of a liquid silvery stream running all the way to the low hills. But this dry country holds promise. Greta, Alec, and Brendan unload the collecting equipment and begin to fan out in different directions.

No rock goes unturned, not even a skull. The skull is that of a horse. A gorgeous iridescent green jumping spider crawls out from a crack, and then a pholcid creeps from the eye socket. It is a skull of life, not death. Greta pops the two spiders into separate vials and takes a reading on her GPS to mark the location. Minutes later, she discovers three spiders under one rock—a tarantula, a jumping spider, and a spitting spider. She puts the jumping and the spitting spiders into vials, but not the tarantula. Greta adores tarantulas. With their hairy bodies, they remind her of teddy bears. This one has blue legs. But they come in all colors, from gold to lilac. She holds this one in her hands for a minute or so, and then she gently releases this animal to go back to its retreat. Greta is against collecting tarantulas, since many are endangered due to poachers who sell them to hobbyists.

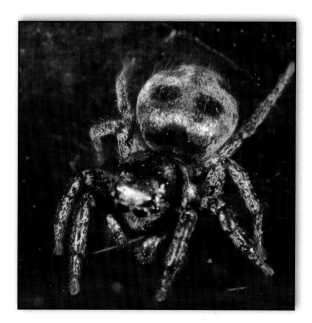

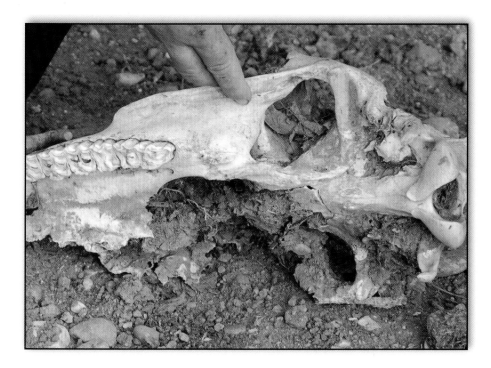

The iridescent jumping spider (top) is much smaller than the tarantula (bottom).

Then, against a rocky outcropping sprigged with dry prickly plants, Greta spies a bluish mist, almost like a miniature fog bank emerging from a crack. It's the web of a *Loxosceles*. Can the creature be far away? Seconds later, she sees the occupant. A *Loxosceles* at last! Wild cheers erupt. Greta and her two students high-five each other.

It is an immature female, and Greta is almost positive it is an *L. taino*. If so, it will be the first time one has been found in the northwest country of the Dominican Republic. Like most scientists, Greta delights in "firsts." However, before she can confirm its species as *L. taino*, she will have to examine it under a microscope.

She continues searching and begins to follow a gully now. There is a cliff ahead, not a high one, but barbed wire runs along it. She climbs quickly to the top and spots some *Loxosceles* molts poking out from under rocks on the other side of the fence. She threads her arms through the barbed wire. "I just know they are here," she mutters, and reaches to overturn a rock through the wire. "I roll every rock and look in every crack." Is she afraid of being bitten by not just a brown recluse but a snake or something else? "Nah, I find it peaceful, meditative—rolling rocks."

But soon there is excitement. She discovers another *L. taino*. And not far away, Alec and Brendan find them as well.

This location, at 19°44′169″ North and 71°26′271″ West, is quickly christened Taino Ridge. It took three days, but Greta and her two students have hit the mother lode of *Loxosceles taino*. Three days of dirt, grime, picking through trash and debris, and scrambling over rugged terrain have paid off.

Greta bursts into song. "Oh, *Lox! Lox! Loxosoceles* . . . " Her voice goes higher as she climbs an operatic scale, jumping octaves as easily as a spider might ascend its silken web. She dances around a bit. She was, after all, Miss Cheerleader for the state of Indiana when she was in high school. She must dance! She must sing! For at this moment, Greta Binford is simply delirious with the joy of discovery.

The Deadliest of All Deadlies

In late afternoon, Greta, Alec, and Brendan pack up to leave. By the time they are on the road, night has fallen. Greta is driving the van back to Puerto Plata. More deadly than any spider toxin, the biggest threat in the Dominican Republic, the danger that is most likely to kill you, is driving at night. The roads are terrible. There are few regulations concerning traffic or cars. Many cars in this poor country drive with damaged headlights, or none at all. The roads often do not have a stripe down them. And flimsy motorbikes with no reflectors zip about like gnats on a summer night. It is terrifying.

Three hours later, however, Greta arrives at the modest hotel where she and the two students are staying. The proprietor welcomes them back warmly. He does not know what Greta and her students carry in the coolers, or what they have already stashed in Greta's room. He might find it alarming, as would the other guests, if he knew that the coolers contained half a dozen black widows, as well as perhaps two dozen *Loxosceles*, or brown recluse spiders.

Up close and personal with two Loxosceles.
Top: A female

Bottom: A female that recently molted

That night, before she goes to bed, Greta takes out the vials of various spiders and ponders them—not greedily, as a miser might contemplate her gold, but blissfully, for what she can now share with the world. She is overwhelmed by these treasures, the sheer beauty that she finds often deep in people's trash and in the rot of nature. She imagines the lovely delicacy of the *Leucauge*'s web, the stunning symmetry of its spiraling radiations of silk; the glistening colors of the jumping spider, with its bright blue abdomen; and then there is the other jumping spider, like an emerald chip, that she collected from the death head of the horse skull. There is no horror, no ugliness. The red-orange *Chrysso* looks like a brilliant jewel in the plastic vial. The memory of the tarantula with its purple and magenta sheen reminds her of a glowing twilight. "It's like opening a Christmas present to find a tarantula," Greta says softy. She sighs. "Just like Christmas."

Glossary of Spiders

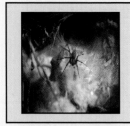

Agelenopsis sp.*

Common name:
grass spider

page 22

Anasaitis sp.*

Common name:
jumping spider

page 51

  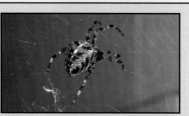

Araneus diadematus

Common name:
European garden spider

pages 13, 62, 63

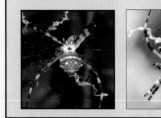

Argiope argentata

Common name:
silver Argiope

pages 3, 7

Chrysso sp.*

page 46

Coras americanus

Common name:
funnel-web spider

page 28

Gasterocantha cancriformes

Common name:
spiny orb weaver, jewel spider

pages 12, 39

Latrodectus geometricus

Common name:
brown widow

page 49

Leucauge venusta

Common name:
orchard spider

page 26

* *sp.* indicates species undescribed

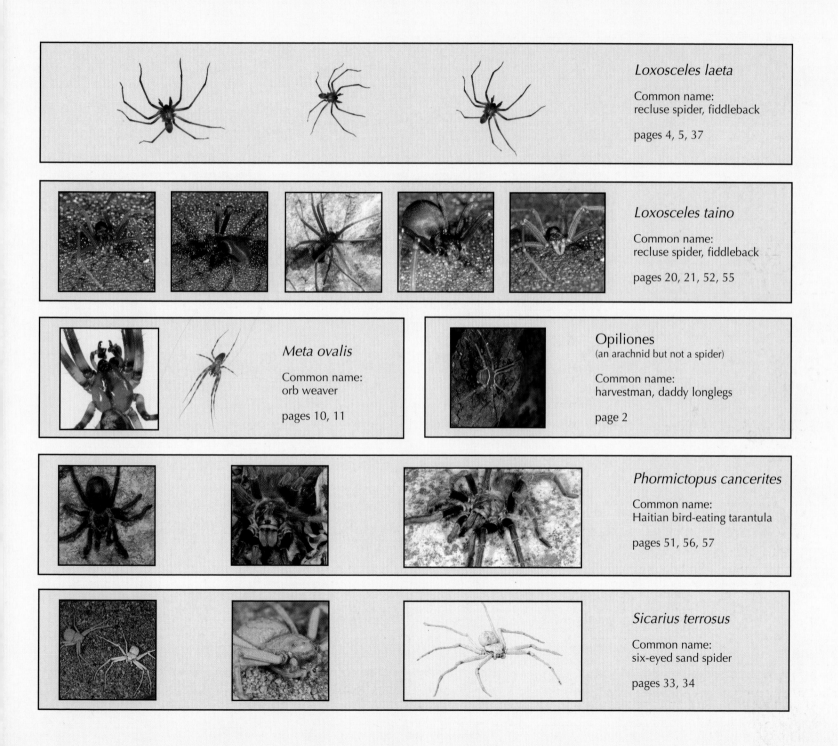

Loxosceles laeta

Common name:
recluse spider, fiddleback

pages 4, 5, 37

Loxosceles taino

Common name:
recluse spider, fiddleback

pages 20, 21, 52, 55

Meta ovalis

Common name:
orb weaver

pages 10, 11

Opiliones
(an arachnid but not a spider)

Common name:
harvestman, daddy longlegs

page 2

Phormictopus cancerites

Common name:
Haitian bird-eating tarantula

pages 51, 56, 57

Sicarius terrosus

Common name:
six-eyed sand spider

pages 33, 34

Sources

Books

Bishop, Nic. *Spiders*. New York: Scholastic, 2007.

Dalton, Stephen. *Spiders, The Ultimate Predators*. Buffalo, NY: Firefly Books, 2008.

Foelix, Rainer F. *The Biology of Spiders*. 2nd edition. New York: Oxford University Press, 1996.

Gertsch, Willis John. *American Spiders*. New York: Van Nostrand Reinhold, 1979.

Hillyard, Paul. *The Private Life of Spiders*. Princeton, NJ: Princeton University Press, 2008.

Levi, Herbert and Lorna. *Spiders and Their Kin*. New York: Golden Press, 1968.

Schnieper, Claudia; photographs by Max Meirer. *Amazing Spiders*. Minneapolis: Carolrhoda Books, 1989.

Ubick, D., P. Paquin, P. E. Cushing, and V. Roth, eds. *Spiders of North America*: *An Identification Manual*. Keene, NH: American Arachnological Society, 2005.

Websites

American Arachnological Society
http://www.americanarachnology.org

Greta Binford's website
http://legacy.lclark.edu/~binford/

Tree of Life Web Project/Arachnid Branch
http://www.tolweb.org/Arachnida

The World Spider Catalog at the American Museum of Natural History, New York
http://research.amnh.org/iz/spiders/catalog/INTRO1.html

Index

Page numbers in italics indicate illustrations.